D1561169

THE FORMER SOVIET UNION:
THEN AND NOW

The South Caucasus: Then and Now

Michael V. Uschan

ReferencePoint Press®

ReferencePoint Press®

About the Author

Michael V. Uschan has written more than ninety books, including *Life of an American Soldier in Iraq,* for which he won the 2005 Council for Wisconsin Writers Juvenile Nonfiction Award. It was the second time he won the award. Uschan began his career as a writer and editor with United Press International, a wire service that provided stories to newspapers, radio, and television. He and his wife, Barbara, reside in the Milwaukee suburb of Franklin, Wisconsin.

© 2015 ReferencePoint Press, Inc.
Printed in the United States

For more information, contact:
ReferencePoint Press, Inc.
PO Box 27779
San Diego, CA 92198
www.ReferencePointPress.com

Picture Credits
Accurate Art, Inc.: Cover, 8, © Ina Fassbender/Reuters/Corbis: 55, © Gleb Garanich/Reuters/Corbis: 47, © Antoine Gyori/AGP/Corbis: 27, © Heritage Images/Corbis: 17, © Jeremy Homer/Corbis: 60, © Daniel Lainé/Corbis: 31, © Photolure/Itar-Tass/Corbis: 64, © Jose Fuste Raga/Corbis: 67, © Michael Runkel/Robert Harding World Imagery/Corbis: 52, Thinkstock Images: 4, 5, 23, Yvan Travert/akg-images/Newscom: 42, © Peter Turnley/Corbis: 36, T1230 Plank bridge in a deep gorge in the Caucasus Mountains, c.1860, Premazzi, Luigi (Ludwig Osipovich) (1814–91)/© Royal Geographical Society, London, UK/The Bridgeman Art Library: 13

LIBRARY OF CONGRESS CATALOGING-IN-PUBLICATION DATA

Uschan, Michael V., 1948- author.
  The South Caucasus : then and now / by Michael V. Uschan.
      pages ; cm. -- (The Former Soviet Union: then and now)
   ISBN-13: 978-1-60152-650-2 (hardback)
   ISBN-10: 1-60152-650-4 (hardback)
  1. Caucasus, South--History--20th century. 2. Caucasus, South--Relations--Soviet Union.
  3. Soviet Union--Relations--Caucasus, South. I. Title. II. Series: Former Soviet Union--then and now.
   DK509.U83 2015
   947.5084--dc23

                                                                2013041613

CONTENTS

IMPORTANT EVENTS IN THE SOUTH CAUCASUS: THEN AND NOW

1918
World War I ends; Georgia, Azerbaijan, and Armenia declare themselves independent republics.

1965
Armenians mark the fiftieth anniversary of the Armenian genocide with protests.

1828
Through a treaty with Persia, the Russian Empire gains control of most of Azerbaijan and half of Armenia.

1924
An armed uprising against Soviet rule in Georgia is the last in any South Caucasus country.

1990
Armenia declares its independence from the Soviet Union.

1830   1920   1940   1960   1980

1989
Twenty people are killed during an anti-Soviet demonstration in Tbilisi, Georgia.

1922
The Union of Soviet Socialist Republics is created; Armenia, Azerbaijan, and Georgia enter it together as the Transcaucasian Socialist Federative Soviet Republic.

1945
World War II ends; nearly 2 million South Caucasians fought in the conflict and more than 700,000 died.

1936
Armenia, Azerbaijan, and Georgia become separate Soviet republics.

1991
Georgia and Azerbaijan each declare their independence from the Soviet Union.

4

1992
Armenia and Azerbaijan fight over Nagorno-Karabakh, which wants to secede from Azerbaijan.

1995
Armenians approve a constitution guaranteeing citizens various rights, including the right to vote; Eduard Shevardnadze becomes Georgia's first president.

2004
Mikheil Saakashvili is elected president of Georgia, and an era of greater democracy begins.

1999
Six government officials, including prime minister Vazgen Sargsyan, are killed in an armed attack on the Armenian Parliament.

2008
Georgia and Russia fight a five-day war over control of South Ossetia.

1995   **2000**   **2005**   **2010**   **2015**

2001
Georgia and Abkhazia sign a nonaggression pact; Azerbaijan begins using the Latin alphabet.

2013
Serzh Sargsyan is elected to a second term as president of Armenia; Ilham Aliyev is elected to a third term as president of Azerbaijan.

1994
A cease-fire ends a war between Armenia and Azerbaijan over Nagorno-Karabakh; Azerbaijan signs the "Contract of the Century" to supply oil to oil companies around the world.

1993
Georgians are driven out of Abkhazia by residents who want to secede from Georgia.

Gateway to Asia

The South Caucasus region includes three countries—Armenia, Azerbaijan, and Georgia—that were former republics of the Union of Soviet Socialist Republics (USSR). The name *South Caucasus* is derived from their geographical relationship to the Caucasus, a towering mountain range slotted between the Black Sea and the Caspian Sea. The Caucasus, the entire area's dominant physical feature, drifts southward west to east in a line that is 680 miles (1,094 km) long and includes Mount Elbrus, which at 18,510 feet (5,642 m) is one of Europe's tallest mountains.

Georgia, the western-most nation in the South Caucasus, is bordered on the north by Russia, on the east by Azerbaijan, on the South by Turkey and Armenia, and on the west by the Black Sea. The Caspian Sea is the eastern border of Azerbaijan and a major source of economic wealth because of that nation's offshore oil wells. Iran curls around Azerbaijan's southern border, and Armenia is its western boundary. Georgia, Azerbaijan, and Turkey surround Armenia, the lone landlocked South Caucasus nation.

On a map, South Caucasus nations look like small pieces of a jigsaw puzzle surrounded by much bigger pieces, which are the far larger and more powerful nations of Russia, Turkey, and Iran. The natural geography that placed this trio of countries between several powerful nations with widely divergent cultures, religions, and ideals has been the most important factor in their long history. And much of that history has been detrimental to people inhabiting the South Caucasus.

A Bitter Battleground

The location of the three countries has been key to their history because they sit on the crossroads between Europe and Asia. As a result, historian

Besik Urigashvili states, "The 'gateway' to Asia has never been peaceful and [the] history of the region is the history of conquests, wars, and civil conflicts."[1] For several thousand years, control of the South Caucasus was contested by armies of the Persian, Turkish, Arab, Mongol, and Russian Empires, all of which at one time swept through and controlled all or parts of the South Caucasus. Those powers fought for the area because it was the main trade route between Europe and Asia, which meant riches for whoever controlled it.

The South Caucasus also became a battleground for cultures of the countries competing to control it. During the succession of wars and periods of rule by the various nations or groups of people that continually washed over the South Caucasus for several thousand years, the cultures of the conquerors and the conquered became intertwined. As a result, more than fifty different ethnic groups inhabit the South Caucasus today. They speak a wide variety of languages, and their many unique cultural heritages have left them with many differences in how they live—from the food they eat to the music they dance to.

> "The 'gateway' to Asia has never been peaceful and [the] history of the region is the history of conquests, wars, and civil conflicts."[1]
>
> —Historian Besik Urigashvili.

Religion is the cultural issue that has most often historically divided people of the South Caucasus. Armenia in 301 became the first nation to adopt Christianity as its state religion, and Georgia soon followed. Azerbaijan, however, is an Islamic nation. At various times in history, forces devoted to one religion have dominated areas inhabited by those of the other faith. Animosity grew out of the harsh way conquerors sometimes dealt with members of other religions. In 1915, for example, Turkey's Islamic Ottoman Empire (which then ruled Armenia) killed an estimated 1.5 million Christian Armenians in what has come to be known as the Armenian Genocide.

Russia Conquers the South Caucasus

In modern times Russia has been the major power in the South Caucasus. Portions of all three countries were part of the Russian Empire from the

The South Caucasus

Greater Caucasus Mountains

Russian Federation

Abkhazia

Caspian Sea

Black Sea

South Ossetia

Georgia

● Tbilisi

Turkey

Armenia

Azerbaijan

● Yerevan

Baku ●

Nagorno-Karabakh

Azerbaijan

Iran

early 1800s until 1917, when Communists seized power from Nicholas II, the last Russian czar. After a brief period of independence following the emperor's overthrow, all three nations were forced to join the USSR in the early 1920s, when its army invaded and conquered them.

Soviet rule drastically transformed South Caucasus nations by imposing Communist economic policies that included eliminating private ownership of farms, which had been the way of life for most people. The Soviets also tried to force people to give up religious, cultural, and ethnic beliefs to standardize life throughout the USSR.

The three nations became independent in 1991 when the USSR broke apart. All three countries have fared well since then, adopting democratic systems of government and building strong economies. However, the region's historic instability due to religious and ethnic differences continues to haunt the South Caucasus.

More Fighting

Communist rule was so forceful that it prevented ancient religious and ethnic rivalries from flaring up. However, since 1991, historic resentments and prejudices have again beset the area. For example, the Communists had forced Abkhazia and South Ossetia, two small ethnic areas, to be part of Georgia. But in 1991 when the Soviet Union fell apart, the two declared their independence from Georgia in a tense situation that has often flared into violence. And in 2008 when Georgia invaded South Ossetia, military forces from Russia—the powerful remnant of the former Soviet Union—stepped in to keep Georgia from overpowering it. Relations between Georgia and the two republics as well as Georgia and Russia have remained tense since then.

Another example of the historic rivalries that continue to plague the South Caucasus since the Soviet Union's demise is the ongoing fight between Azerbaijan and Armenia over control of the Nagorno-Karabakh region of southwestern Azerbaijan. The conflict is based on religion and ethnicity; Azerbaijan is an Islamic country, but a majority of people who lived in that region were ethnic Armenians who were Christian. This battle even erupted into an undeclared war from 1988 to 1994 in the disputed mountainous region. The area internationally is considered part of Azerbaijan. However, Armenian residents primarily control it and call it the Nagorno-Karabakh Republic, a status only three nations recognize. Thus ancient animosities have, once again, brought strife to the South Caucasus despite the new economic prosperity and freer way of life its people enjoy.

CHAPTER ONE

Soviet Union Domination

South Caucasus is the name most commonly applied to the region that includes Georgia, Armenia, and Azerbaijan, but it has also been called Transcaucus, Transcaucasia, and Transcaucasus. Tamaz Gamkrelidze, an internationally known linguist, says that *South Caucasus* is the most correct designation for the area because it places the area in its geographic relationship to the Caucasus Mountains. This range serves as both a dividing line and physical pathway between Europe and Asia.

The region's location placed it between more powerful nations and empires, including Russia, Turkey, and Iran, which throughout its long history repeatedly invaded South Caucasus countries and warred with other powers to control the area. Historian A.O. Sarkissian explains that the resulting bloodshed grew out of a clash of opposing religions, cultures, and traditions all seeking to dominate the South Caucasus: "Geographically the Transcaucasian region forms a bridge between East and West, between Asia and Europe. [It] has been a perpetual battleground of opposing civilizations and of invading armies [and each] of the conquering powers left the imprints of its particular civilization upon the inhabitants of the land."[2]

Conquerors who invaded and ruled parts of the South Caucasus include noted historic figures Genghis Khan, Alexander the Great, and Peter the Great; the latter in the early eighteenth century having created the Russian Empire. That history of domination continued in the early twentieth century when the USSR used military force to seize Georgia, Armenia, and Azerbaijan. Because they were surrounded by much stronger nations, until the modern era all three South Caucasus nations were independent states for only brief periods of time. Despite many centuries of domination, however, each South Caucasus nation has its own unique history and story of cultural accomplishments.

Early History

South Caucasus history began thousands of years ago. Archaeologists believe Azerbaijanis have inhabited that area since the Stone Age. Armenians have been living near the area of Mount Ararat for more than five thousand years, and the ancestors of today's Georgians began living in the area known today as Georgia during the twelfth century BCE.

Armenia is one of the world's oldest civilizations. Armenians claim they are descendants of Hayk, a great-great-grandson of Noah, who according to the Christian Bible built the ark that helped people and animals survive a worldwide flood. Mount Ararat, a towering dormant volcano 16,854 feet (5,137 m) high, is the place on which the Bible claims Noah's ark landed after that flood. Armenia's greatest historical claim is that in 301 it became the first nation to adopt Christianity as its religion.

Although proud of their status as the first Christian nation, Armenians have suffered greatly since then from religious intolerance. Historian Mike Wilson writes, "Beginning in the seventh century, the religion of Islam spread by conquest throughout the lands in which Armenians lived. Armenians went from being citizens in a powerful kingdom to being an oppressed people."[3] A series of Islamic nations ruled Armenia, including the Ottoman Empire, which conquered it in the early sixteenth century and ruled it for the next four hundred years.

Armenia's neighbor, Georgia, is believed to have the longest history of any major nation that was part of the former Soviet Union. One fact

"Beginning in the seventh century, the religion of Islam spread by conquest throughout the lands in which Armenians lived. Armenians went from being citizens in a powerful kingdom to being an oppressed people."[3]

—Historian Mike Wilson.

11

that supports this is that Georgian is a unique language that is not related to any other family of European or Asian languages spoken in the area. Georgia even has its own unique alphabet of thirty-three letters unlike those of any other writing system. Like Armenia, Georgia in 337 also adopted Christianity as its state religion. Both nations remained Christian despite being conquered over the centuries by Islamic countries, as was neighboring Azerbaijan, itself a Muslim nation. Azerbaijan adopted Sunni Islam in the seventh century, when Arabs controlled it.

Azerbaijan's name is derived from two Persian words—*azer*, which means "fire," and *baijan*, which translates as either "guardian" or "protector." The name comes from flames that were produced when natural gas and oil seeped to the surface and sometimes erupted into flames. The energy sources that helped give Azerbaijan its name today make it rich through their sales.

Arabs were just one group that over the long history of the South Caucasus kept invading and conquering Armenia, Azerbaijan, and Georgia. In the first century BCE, the Roman Empire ruled most of the area, and in the centuries that followed, Turkish, Mongolian, and Persian armies overwhelmed the small countries. In the nineteenth century Russia began its long, harsh rule over the South Caucasus, first by the Russian Empire and then by the Soviet Union. The South Caucasus, however, was just a small part of the Russian Empire, one of the largest empires that has ever existed.

The Russian Empire

The Russian Empire in the early nineteenth century ruled more than 125 million people in a vast area extending from Europe all the way to the empire's southern border with China. For much of that century, the Russian Empire contended with the Ottoman (Turkey) and Persian (Iran) Empires in a series of wars over the South Caucasus. Slowly, the Russians won control of the area.

Georgia, the closest geographically to the Russian Empire, was the first one to be absorbed. Although the Russians simply wanted to expand their territory and power, they claimed they had another, more

A plank bridge crosses a raging river in this nineteenth-century painting of the Caucasus Mountains. The three countries that make up the South Caucasus—Armenia, Azerbaijan, and Georgia—lie in the shadow of the Caucasus Mountains.

Oil Was a Source of Wealth

The biggest source of Azerbaijan's economic wealth today comes from the sale of oil and natural gas. Those riches started pouring into Azerbaijan in 1846 when that country became the first in the world to drill an oil well, which was located near Baku. Up until drilling began, people had only been able to collect oil by digging shallow wells in the ground to allow oil to flow to the surface. An October 28, 1900, story in the *New York Times* gave a glowing account of how the influx of oil money had changed the city: "Baku has acquired considerable wealth, and the city, which has naturally extended in all directions, contains substantially built, indeed elegant, stone houses and large shops, which would do credit to any city of Europe. Evidences of wealth are not only to be seen in the appearance of the city itself, but also among many of its inhabitants."

Quoted in Nikki Kazimova, *Culture Smart: Azerbaijan.* London: Kuperard, 2011, p. 28.

altruistic purpose. The Russians stated that they sought control of Georgia because Russia, a Christian nation, wanted to protect it from being ruled by the Islamic Ottoman and Persian Empires. When the Russian Empire grew strong enough to challenge its Islamic rivals, it annexed Georgia in 1801.

Russia, however, kept battling Persia for more territory. In 1828 Russia and Persia ended their fighting with the Treaty of Turkmenchay. The terms gave Russia control of most of modern-day Azerbaijan as well as the eastern half of Armenia. Azerbaijan became a prized possession of the Russian Empire because oil became a valuable commodity worldwide in the nineteenth century as a lubricant, source of light, and energy to power machines. In 1846 engineers drilled an oil well 21 feet (6.4 m) deep near the Azerbaijani capital city of Baku, marking the first such well in the history of oil production. It was created more than a decade before Americans began drilling wells in Pennsylvania in 1859.

When World War I started in 1914, South Caucasus countries were still part of either the Russian or Ottoman Empires. But when World War I ended in 1918, the three nations had their first experience of independence in the modern era.

War Leads to Independence

The assassination of Archduke Franz Ferdinand of the Austro-Hungarian Empire on June 28, 1914, ignited World War I. Gavrilo Princip shot him to protest the empire's control of his native Serbia. When the Austro-Hungarian Empire declared war on Serbia a month later, countries like Great Britain, France, and Germany joined in the fighting. They did that because many European countries had made secret alliances to help each other in the event of war. When Austria-Hungary declared war on Serbia, Russia came to its aid. Germany then supported Austria-Hungary, and that set in motion a domino effect of other countries coming to the aid of friendly nations.

Initially, the Allies—France, Great Britain, Belgium, and Russia—fought the Central Powers of Germany, Austria-Hungary, and the Ottoman Empire. When fighting spread to colonies the various nations had in Africa, Asia, and the Pacific, the conflict turned into history's first global war. The entry of the United States into the war on the side of the Allies in April 1917 was decisive in helping the Allies win.

The war ended on November 11, 1918, but its effect on the world had only just begun. During the conflict Russians became angry with Czar Nicholas II because he continued to deny citizens most rights, and most people were poor. Russian citizens were also upset about fighting a war they did not support. The Communists used that discontent to oust the czar. The collapse of the Russian Empire and the Austro-Hungarian and Ottoman Empires at the end of the war allowed countries they had ruled to become independent. The new nations included Georgia, Armenia, and Azerbaijan. Their independence, however, would last only a short time before they would be conquered once again by Russia, which by this time was governed by Communists.

Brief Freedom

All three South Caucasus nations declared their independence in May 1918 while Communists were still battling for complete control of Russia. In the next few years, the three countries had varied experiences as independent nations. All of them, however, became involved in military clashes as they and other nations sought to claim South Caucasus territory.

On May 26, 1918, Georgia declared itself the Democratic Republic of Georgia. As in czarist Russia, members of royalty and people of wealth owned most of the land. The republic's new government initiated land reform that made it possible for many more people to own small tracts of land. This was vitally important in a country in which most people lived in rural areas and made their living as farmers. The republic also had a multiparty system to elect officials and was trying to make life better for most people. Historian Ronald G. Suny writes, "Their achievement in building a Georgian political nation was extraordinary."[4] It was remarkable because it was the first time in centuries that Georgia had been a separate entity not ruled by a foreign power.

> "Their achievement in building a Georgian political nation was extraordinary."[4]
>
> —Historian Ronald G. Suny.

The Azerbaijan Democratic Republic also made impressive strides in creating a better way to govern its people after centuries of having being ruled by royal empires. The republic marked the first attempt to establish a secular and democratic nation in the Muslim world. In that period Islamic nations were all ruled by royal dynasties, and as in the Russian Empire, citizens of these nations had few legal rights and little say in how they were governed. Historian Aslan Amani writes that this was a bold historical event for Azerbaijan: "Azerbaijan democratic republic was the first parliamentary democracy, republican form of governance in the Muslim world."[5] One of the democratic reforms it initiated was to give women the right to vote; it was the first Muslim country and one of the first in the world to grant women that right.

The new Republic of Armenia also established a democratic form of government, an important step after centuries of rule by Russia and other powers. The process of setting up a new government included organizing an army. And on June 30, 1918, Armenians chose Hovhannes Katchaznouni as prime minister and elected legislators who for the first time in Armenia's history could make laws governing the populace.

The newly independent South Caucasus countries, however, could not escape the lingering effects of hatred that had long existed between them due to centuries-old clashes over territory in their region. Thus, Georgia,

An angry mob storms the czar's winter palace in 1917 during the Russian Revolution. The revolution that ousted the czar led to a brief period of independence for Georgia, Azerbaijan, and Armenia.

Armenia, and Azerbaijan all began their periods of independence by battling each other over their respective borders. Georgia and Armenia fought a series of several small battles in December 1918, and fighting ended only when Great Britain helped the two sides agree to a cease-fire. And Azerbaijan became embroiled in a war with neighboring Armenia over territory they both claimed. A major reason for the war was Azerbaijan's oil reserves, an increasingly valuable economic commodity in the modern world. Armenia's future was further threatened militarily by the remnants of the Ottoman Empire, which invaded it in 1920 and was trying to extend its borders into the South Caucasus. The attempt resulted in a full-scale war, fueled by religious differences between Christian Armenia and Islamic Turkey, which became a nation in 1923.

"Azerbaijan democratic republic was the first parliamentary democracy, republican form of governance in the Muslim world."[5]

—Historian Aslan Amani.

The unsettled political and military conditions following World War I, which included battles between all three South Caucasus countries, greatly weakened the region. And that made the countries ripe for invasion by the Communists, who were determined to regain control of the Russian Empire's former territories after winning control of Russia.

The Soviet Union

Azerbaijan was the first South Caucasus country forced to join the Soviet Union. The Soviet Union desperately wanted Azerbaijan because it needed the country's oil supplies. In a telegram on March 17, 1920, Communist leader Vladimir Lenin ordered army units in the South Caucasus to invade Azerbaijan and seize Baku, its capital. On April 25 the Eleventh Red Army crossed into and took control of Azerbaijan, immediately dissolved its Parliament, and named new officials to run the nation. Nariman Narimanov, who headed the Azerbaijan Communist Party, was named as president. On April 28, 1920, the new government declared the nation part of the Soviet Union and changed the country's name to the Azerbaijan Soviet Socialist Republic.

Genocide in Armenia

April 24 is known as Genocide Remembrance Day in Armenia. This day commemorates the systematic killing and deportation of Armenians from an area in the Ottoman Empire that had once been part of Armenia. Christian Armenians had always faced discrimination from Islamic nations that ruled them, and this religious rivalry had sometimes resulted in violence against Armenians. In 1915 the Ottoman Empire feared that Armenian Christians would join the Russian Empire in fighting it during World War I. To stop that threat, the Ottomans began to force Armenians to leave and killed many more. No one knows how many people suffered in what Armenians call *Mets Yegherrn*, Armenian for "Great Crime." Estimates by historians vary greatly on the number of Armenians who were killed and range from 600,000 to 1.5 million. Historical reports claim the Turks murdered large groups of Armenians through burning or drowning, in forced death marches, and in extermination camps. British prime minister Winston Churchill once explained his views on why the Ottomans committed such a horrendous crime: "In 1915 the Turkish Government began and ruthlessly carried out the infamous general massacre and deportation of Armenians. [There] is no reasonable doubt that this crime was planned and executed for political reasons. The opportunity presented itself for clearing Turkish soil of a Christian race opposed to all Turkish ambitions."

Winston Churchill, *The World Crisis*, vol. 5. New York: Scribner, 1929, p. 342.

Faced with new efforts by Turkey to take over Armenia, Armenia's leaders willingly joined the Soviet Union in the belief that their country would fare better under Communist rule than under Turkish rule. Historian Paul D. Steeves writes, "On November 19, 1920, the Armenians accepted the status of a Soviet Socialist Republic to secure Russian protection."[6] Linking with the Soviets had mixed results. After Armenia joined the Soviet Union, it signed a treaty with Turkey to end their war.

However, the Treaty of Alexandropol gave Turkey territory in Armenia that the old Ottoman Empire had controlled. The land included the medieval Armenian capital of Ani as well as Mount Ararat, a spiritual icon for Armenians. The Soviets further reduced Armenia's borders by giving other parts of it to Azerbaijan, including the area of Nagorno-Karabakh, which Armenia still claims as its own today.

Unlike the other two South Caucasus countries, Georgia had adopted communism during its brief period of independence. The Social Democratic Labor Party, which was Communist, had won nearly 82 percent of the vote in the 1919 elections for Parliament. However, Georgia's brand of communism differed from that of Russia by allowing multiple political parties and greater freedom for its citizens. Georgia's style of communism, however, placed it at odds with another group of Communists who began waging a fight for control of the Communist Party. The two groups of Communists were called Bolsheviks and Mensheviks. The split that resulted in these two groups occurred in Russia in 1903. Both groups supported political and economic reforms that would end domination of average people by royalty and the wealthy, but they differed on many other issues. The key difference was that the Bolsheviks believed a small group of professional revolutionaries should be making decisions, whereas the Mensheviks wanted more party members to share in the decision making.

The battle for control of the Russian Communist Party ultimately ended with a Bolshevik victory. And it was the Bolsheviks, led by the Georgia native Joseph Stalin, who invaded Georgia on February 2, 1921. On February 25 the Red Army entered the Georgian capital of Tbilisi and installed its own Communist government led by Georgian Filipp Makharadze, who agreed to join the Soviet Union.

The independence the three South Caucasus nations experienced was all too brief. And for the next seven decades, they would be subjected to the harsh, often brutal way in which the Soviet Union governed such conquered nations.

CHAPTER TWO

Political Life in the South Caucasus

The USSR was born on December 30, 1922, when member countries approved a treaty creating it. Armenia, Azerbaijan, and Georgia entered the USSR as the Transcaucasian Socialist Federative Soviet Republic. Placing them into one political entity was not a new idea; it had been tried unsuccessfully at the end of World War I. In April 1917 after Communists overthrew the Russian Empire, Georgians tried to persuade the other two nations to join them in a proposed Transcaucasian Democratic Federative Republic. However, by the end of May 1918 the three had all declared their independence as separate countries.

Armenia, grateful to be spared more brutality at the hands of Islamic Turks, and Azerbaijan, whose oil riches were key to the republic's economic future, were generally happy with the arrangement. But Georgians were angry because it took away their right to rule themselves. Political opposition to Soviet domination grew and culminated in an August 1924 uprising to overthrow Soviet rule. The fighting lasted until September, when the Red Army and a force led by Georgia native Joseph Stalin crushed the uprising and punished Georgians with violent reprisals.

A newspaper report claimed that after entering Georgia's capital of Tbilisi, Soviet soldiers executed six hundred of the city's leading citizens and imprisoned hundreds of other people. It is believed that as many as ten thousand people were killed to punish the uprising. Historian Iurii Trifonov writes that the uprising's violent aftermath ended South Caucasus opposition to communism: "[The 1924] revolt in Georgia [was] the last major outbreak of armed counterrevolution in the Transcaucasus, a vain attempt to split the Soviet system from within and to tear Georgia from [Soviet control]."[7] South Caucasus nations would not regain their independence until the Soviet Union fell apart seven decades later.

Communist Brutality

The Communist Party made and enforced laws for the Soviet Union, which made it a totalitarian form of government. In 1922 Stalin became general secretary of the Communist Party and the Soviet Union's most powerful leader. To ensure South Caucasus countries would obey the new regime, Stalin began a brutal campaign that included deporting opponents to work camps in harsh areas like Siberia and imprisoning and murdering tens of thousands of people he deemed a danger to Communist rule, including intellectuals and members of royalty.

> "[The 1924] revolt in Georgia [was] the last major outbreak of armed counterrevolution in the Transcaucasus, a vain attempt to split the Soviet system from within and to tear Georgia from [Soviet control]."[7]
>
> —Historian Iurii Trifonov.

Stalin dealt more ruthlessly with his homeland than with other Soviet republics. In the first few years of Soviet rule, about 50,000 Georgians were executed and more than 150,000 jailed or forced to leave. This brutal treatment often seemed random and senseless. For example, everyone named Paniashvili in the Georgian village of Ruisi was executed because one person with that name had been involved in the 1924 revolt.

Stalin was especially harsh with members of royalty. He once asked Lavrenty Beria, head of the Soviet Union's dreaded secret police, what percentage of Georgia's royal class was still alive. When Beria told him it was about 3 percent, Stalin replied, "Make that number be zero percent."[8] Stalin used similar violent methods to make people in Armenia and Azerbaijan accept Soviet rule.

After eliminating opposition in all three countries, on December 5, 1936, Stalin broke up the Transcaucasian Republic and allowed the countries to become individual Soviet republics. Stalin's brutal control over the Soviet Union continued until he died in 1953. His death marked the beginning of a new Communist era for South Caucasus nations in which they gradually gained more individual freedom and local control.

Soviet Georgia

Under Stalin the USSR's Communist Party made laws and set policies for the republics. When Nikita Khrushchev succeeded Stalin, he decentralized power to make it easier for republics to pass laws and approve programs that helped their residents. However, some government officials began using their new power to enrich themselves by making people pay bribes to win government contracts or split profits with officials. Historians Carolyn McGiffert Ekedahl and Melvin A. Goodman write, "Georgia [had] a reputation second to none [for government corruption] and in Georgia it seems to have been carried out on an unparalleled scale and with unrivaled scope and daring."[9]

Although a native of Georgia, Joseph Stalin showed no mercy for his compatriots. As leader of the Soviet Union, Stalin demonstrated extreme brutality toward Georgians and millions of other people who lived under Soviet control.

Illegal dealings in Georgia became so blatant that in 1973 national officials removed Vasil Mzhavanadze as head of the Georgia Communist Party and replaced him with Eduard Shevardnadze, who had a reputation for fighting corruption. Shevardnadze cleaned up government affairs by firing hundreds of crooked officials. In 1985, he was promoted to minister of foreign affairs for the Soviet Union and replaced by Jumber Patiashvili. But Patiashvili was a weak leader and was unable to contend with a growing desire by Georgians for more political and social freedom.

History's Greatest Mass Murderer

Joseph Stalin is remembered as one of the most infamous mass murderers in history. Because of a lack of records, it is impossible to know how many deaths Stalin caused. Historians believe he was responsible for killing at least 20 million people, a figure much higher than German dictator Adolf Hitler is believed responsible for, and some claim the number was much higher. Stalin is blamed for millions of deaths in the 1920s, when he brutally repressed any opposition to Communist takeover of countries, including Armenia, Azerbaijan, and Georgia. The deaths were due to military battles, executions, torture, imprisonment, and deportation to work camps where people were brutally treated. Many of Stalin's political enemies died while being tortured to make them confess to made-up crimes, and he often watched, urging torturers to beat their victims even more severely. Stalin's daughter, Svetlana Alliluyeva, once said, "My father gave his name to the bloodbath of absolute dictatorship. He knew what he was doing. He was neither insane nor misled. With cold calculation he cemented his own power, afraid of losing it more than anything else in the world."

Quoted in H. Montgomery Hyde, *Stalin: The History of a Dictator*. New York: Farrar, Straus and Giroux, 1971, p. 609.

The new political mood in Georgia was bolstered by perestroika—a Russian word meaning "restructuring"—which Mikhail Gorbachev had started in 1985 after he became head of the Soviet Communist Party. He allowed republics more political freedom and let them initiate reforms that moved their economies away from communism, in which the government owns and operates all businesses, toward capitalism, in which people own and operate them. The new freedoms sharply increased nationalism and a desire for independence in the people.

In the late 1980s Georgians began holding public protests demanding freedom from the Soviet Union. On April 9, 1989, an anti-Soviet demonstration in Tbilisi was brutally repressed by the Soviet Army; twenty protesters died and hundreds of others were injured. Most victims were women and children, including a sixteen-year-old girl whom soldiers beat to death.

The incident increased opposition to Soviet rule, and on October 28, 1990, Georgia held multiparty elections for the first time since becoming a Soviet republic. Anti-Soviet feelings continued to strengthen, and on April 9, 1991, the second anniversary of the Tbilisi incident, 98.9 percent of Georgians voted to leave the Soviet Union. The Soviet Union was so weak that it could not stop Georgia from becoming independent.

The Rose Revolution

Independence for the Republic of Georgia was followed by a bitter struggle for political control that lasted several years and erupted briefly into civil war. On May 26, 1991, Zviad Gamsakhurdia was elected president. He had become popular by fighting for independence and civil rights such as freedom of religion. But he quickly alienated Georgians with the dictatorial way he governed and by January 1992 was forced to leave the country. In March 1992 leaders of several groups that had ousted Gamsakhurdia asked Shevardnadze to return, and he assumed the post of president without an election. Gamsakhurdia, claiming to be Georgia's rightful leader, returned on September 24, 1993, with an armed force and captured control of much of western Georgia. The brief civil war ended on December 31 when Gamsakhurdia committed suicide in the village of Khibula as Georgian soldiers were about to capture him.

"Georgia [had] a reputation second to none [for government corruption] and in Georgia it seems to have been carried out on an unparalleled scale and with unrivaled scope and daring."[9]

—Historians Carolyn McGiffert Ekedahl and Melvin A. Goodman.

Russian soldiers helped Shevardnadze against Gamsakhurdia, which weakened his popularity because many Georgians disliked Russian interference with their country. Support for Shevardnadze deteriorated over the next decade due to economic problems, crime, governmental corruption, and his close ties with Russia. When international observers claimed there were voting irregularities in elections for Parliament on November 2, 2003, new protests against Shevardnadze began.

The protests, which became known as the Rose Revolution, led to Shevardnadze's resignation and new elections. Mikheil Saakashvili was elected president, taking office on January 24, 2004. Saakashvili, who served as president for three years and was reelected in 2008 to a five-year term, improved living conditions by eliminating police and government corruption and strengthening the economy.

On August 24, 1995, Georgia ratified a new constitution that strengthened democracy. The constitution affirmed that citizens held ultimate political power, which they exercised through free elections and guaranteed rights that protected them against the government. It also ensured religious freedom by acknowledging the importance of the Georgian Orthodox Church. The constitution made Georgia a democratic republic headed by a president and a prime minister chosen by the president. The parliament of Georgia has 150 members and makes laws for the nation.

The other two South Caucasus countries are also democratic republics. Both experienced difficult times as members of the Soviet Union.

Armenia

The Armenians welcomed the Communists. Many even joined the Eleventh Red Army as it advanced on their country because they were fearful Islamic Turkey would conquer them and resume persecuting Armenian Christians. But during the 1920s and 1930s, tens of thousands of people considered to be anti-Soviet, including writers, artists, political leaders, and members of royalty, were imprisoned, executed, or deported.

So many Armenians were killed during World War II that Stalin invited Armenians who had left the country to escape Turkish or Com-

Hundreds of Georgian students demonstrate at the University of Tbilisi in 2003 during the Rose Revolution. The protests led to the resignation of one president and the election of another.

munist persecution to return. In 1947 and 1948 an estimated 150,000 Armenians came back. Conditions improved under Khrushchev, who made it easier for Christians to practice their religion by loosening controls over the Armenian Church. As had Georgians, Armenians experienced a heightened sense of nationalism. This feeling culminated in mass demonstrations by thousands of people in Yerevan on April 24, 1965, the fiftieth anniversary of the Armenian genocide. Protesters demanded a memorial to the victims, and the government gave in to the demand.

This small victory fed a growing Armenian desire for independence. Protests against Soviet rule began in the late 1980s, and in 1990 the country created the New Armenian Army, a first step toward seeking freedom. On August 23, 1990, Armenia became one of the first republics to declare its independence from the Soviet Union.

The Republic of Armenia

Many historians believe that unity among Armenians due to their bloody past gave it a big advantage over other South Caucasus republics when it became independent. Historians William E. Odom and Robert Dujarric write, "The politics of survival, greatly reinforced by memories of the Turkish massacres of Armenians in 1915, gave Armenia a social and political cohesion unmatched elsewhere in the Transcaucus."[10] That feeling helped Armenia avoid the extreme political divisiveness and ethnic rivalries that plagued Georgia and Azerbaijan. However, Armenian politics were not free from infighting.

> "The politics of survival, greatly reinforced by memories of the Turkish massacres of Armenians in 1915, gave Armenia a social and political cohesion unmatched elsewhere in the Transcaucus."[10]
>
> —Historians William E. Odom and Robert Dujarric.

Armenia has a democratic republic like that of Georgia, headed by a president and with a one-house parliament that makes laws. Levon Ter-Petrosyan was Armenia's president from 1991 to 1998, when he was forced to resign. He was criticized for the country's poor economy, tampering with election results, and banning the Armenian Revolutionary Federation, a political party opposed to him. Robert Kocharyan succeeded him and served until 2008, when Serzh Sargsyan was elected after promising to clean up widespread government corruption he claimed had robbed Armenia of billions of dollars.

Armenian elections, including those for president, have frequently been criticized for voting irregularities and episodes of violence. When Ter-Petrosyan ran again and lost to Sargsyan 53 percent to 21 percent on February 10, 2008, the belief that the election had been rigged ignited a series of protests by tens of thousands of people in Yerevan. At least ten people died in the ensuing violence when soldiers and police broke up the protests, and Ter-Petrosyan was briefly put under house arrest. In 1999 during Kocharyan's presidency, members of the Armenian Revolutionary Federation murdered several leaders of opposition parties

Communist Party Power Structure

In democratic countries the right that citizens have to vote and elect officials of their choice gives them the power to influence decisions at all levels of government. But citizens of Armenia, Azerbaijan, Georgia, and the other Soviet republics did not have that right, because political power was held exclusively by the Communist Party. Individual republics had their own Communist Parties, but they were subordinate to the party's Moscow-based Central Committee.

The Supreme Soviet was the Soviet Union's highest legislative body. Its members were elected by Communist Parties in the various republics on the basis of population and nationality. The existence of the Supreme Soviet gave the appearance of representative government. But in reality a small group of senior officials in the Politburo made all political and economic decisions.

Two members of the Supreme Soviet once admitted to a reporter for the Russian newspaper *Pravda* how little power they had. They commented that party officials in Moscow presented all members with information on the topic at hand and also told them how to vote. All matters, they said, "have essentially been decided in advance," and when it was time to vote, "our vote is invariably unanimous." Thus, citizens and even Communist officials had no real power over how they were governed.

Quoted in Daniel Singer, "All Power to the Soviets," *Nation*, July 30, 1988.

and prime minister Vazgen Sargsyan in what was dubbed the Armenian Parliamentary Shooting.

In Armenia's first few years of independence, it was involved in an undeclared war with neighboring Azerbaijan over Nagorno-Karabakh, an area in Azerbaijan with a majority population of Christian Armenians. The two nations had also battled over the territory in the brief period of independence following World War I but the fighting stopped when both were absorbed into the Soviet Union. The new fighting was sparked by a vote of the Nagorno-Karabakh territorial parliament to become part of Armenia. The fighting began on February 20, 1988, before the collapse of the Soviet Union, and did not end until a cease-fire agreement was reached on May 12, 1994. Armenians won the conflict and expelled more than half a million non-Armenians from the area, which today calls itself the Nagorno-Karabakh Republic even though most nations do not recognize it.

The Azerbaijan Republic

The Red Army invaded Azerbaijan in 1920 for its oil, and on April 18 of that year Azerbaijan became a part of the Soviet Union. The Soviets pumped money into Azerbaijan's oil industry and drilled new wells, and by 1931 Azerbaijan was providing more than 60 percent of Soviet oil. Azerbaijan's oil remained the biggest part of its economy and was vital to the Soviet Union during World War II. But the fact that the Soviet Union benefited more from their oil wealth than Azerbaijanis did angered them and kept alive their desire for independence.

Most Azerbaijanis hated the brutal way Communists had taken over their country and forced them to submit to control from Moscow. However, some Azerbaijanis accepted the reality of the new political situation and joined the Communist Party so they could assume leadership positions in their country. The most powerful and prominent Azerbaijani Soviet leader was Heydar Aliyev.

Free Azerbaijan

The Aliyev family has dominated politics in Azerbaijan for more than four decades. Heydar Aliyev began his rise to power as a member of the Soviet Union's secret police agency that cracked down on opposition to communism. In 1969 Aliyev was appointed head of the Azerbaijan Communist Party to become the nation's top leader and in 1976 was named to the Politburo, which made policy for the entire Soviet Union.

Aliyev was credited with improving the economy and raising the status of Azerbaijan within the Soviet Union. However, he was also accused of having ties to organized crime and profiting from his power. Those claims led Gorbachev to remove him from the Politburo in 1985, and in 1987 Aliyev was forced to give up his position as Azerbaijan's leader because of widespread government corruption.

Azerbaijan's war with Armenia in the late 1980s strengthened nationalism in Azerbaijanis and their desire to become independent. Protesters began demanding freedom from Soviet rule. On January 20, 1990, an estimated 130 protesters were killed in Baku in a confrontation with Soviet troops. The incident, known as Black January, escalated demands for independence, and on August 30, 1991, the Azerbaijan Supreme Soviet voted to become independent.

Ayaz Mutallibov was the first president of the Republic of Azerbaijan but did not stay in power long. Anger over Azerbaijan's loss in the conflict with Armenia forced him to resign on March 6, 1992. Aliyev had remained a powerful behind-the-scenes political force and on June 24, 1993, was elected the republic's third president. He led Azerbaijan until August 4, 2003, when he stepped down due to failing health and named

Oil wells dot the landscape of Baku in Azerbaijan. Azerbaijan's thriving oil industry represented a crucial lifeline for the Soviet Union.

his son, Ilham Aliyev, to replace him. The younger Aliyev has remained in office since.

The Aliyevs provided a sense of political stability for Azerbaijan in the transition from Soviet rule to independence. But the long political dominance of the Aliyevs makes the future of true democracy in Azerbaijan questionable. Some observers have even expressed concern that the family might topple the country's shaky democracy in an effort to hold on to power indefinitely.

Georgia and Armenia both have stronger democracies than Azerbaijan. However, both were still struggling more than two decades after becoming independent to fully understand and implement the full range of principles and safeguards necessary to ensure that their people could enjoy all the benefits of a democratic form of government.

CHAPTER THREE

South Caucasus Economic Life

Communism is an economic system whose name is derived from the Latin word *communis*, a word that means "shared" or "belongs to all." The idea that everyone who lives in a country collectively owns all means of production, from factories to farms, through the state—that is, the government—is at the heart of Communist economic theory. Also under communism, the state had the power to regulate all aspects of economic life, including wages, prices, and even which products are produced. A Communist economic system is directly opposed to capitalism, the economic system that exists in the United States and many other nations. Under capitalism the means of production and other aspects of business are privately owned, and the people who own them, either individuals or a group, make almost all decisions regarding them.

The Communists prevailed in the Russian Revolution largely because members of royalty and a small percentage of people who had become rich through business enterprises held nearly all the wealth in the Russian Empire. Thus, most of the empire's inhabitants were poor and had little hope of improving their lives. This made them eager to support the Communists, who promised that their new economic system would benefit everyone equally instead of enriching only a minority of people.

Like most of the world, Armenia, Azerbaijan, and Georgia had always had capitalist economies. Under Soviet rule, those economies were dismantled and replaced by communism—leading to dramatic changes in daily life for people of the region. Many of those changes made their lives worse instead of better. And when they tried to resist those changes, the Soviet Union brutally punished them.

Communist Ownership

Communist economics in South Caucasus countries started in the 1920s with the new governments in each nation nationalizing businesses, which meant that the state owned and controlled them. This was true of large companies that had built and operated railroads and banks as well as small, single-owner stores that sold food, clothing, and other necessities. The government did not pay owners anything for the property it seized in the name of the state. Former owners were sometimes allowed to work in their old businesses, but their salaries were no greater than that of other workers.

Revolutionary Committees set up in each country handled the initial transformation of South Caucasus economies into Communist ones by taking control of buildings, factories, money, and other property associated with each business. Armenian historian Bagrat Borian wrote in 1929 that the Communists often performed the task of building a new economy brutally and without any regard for the hardships the changes would cause:

> The Revolutionary Committee started a series of indiscriminate seizures and confiscations, without regard to class, and without taking into account the general economic and psychological state of [Armenians]. With amazing recklessness and unconcern, they seized and nationalized everything—military uniforms, artisan tools, rice mills, water mills, barbers' implements, beehives, linen, household furniture, and livestock. [11]

All important economic decisions during the Soviet era were made in Moscow and were meant to benefit the Soviet Union as a whole. The problem was that those decisions often hurt local economic interests in the various republics. The Soviets also made those decisions without regard for how individuals would be affected. For example, they transformed large mansions with multiple rooms that a single rich family had owned into public housing for many other people. And food, from vegetables to meat, was portioned out so everyone would have enough food to eat. The Communist goal was to make people equal in what they had. Although that helped poor people who had never had decent housing or enough to eat, it reduced the lifestyle of people who had once had more. And Communist officials often used their power to secure better housing, food, and other comforts than the rest of the population.

Communist Changes

The group that lost the most was farmers. In the period when South Caucasus nations became Soviet republics, most people lived in rural areas and worked in agriculture. The Soviets seized farms from private individuals and organized them into two types of government-run farms. A kolkhoz was a collective farm owned by the state that was worked by multiple men and women. A sovkhoz was also a collective farm but was much bigger and on average had nearly seventy-six hundred workers. Communist officials operated both types of farms, dictating the crops to be grown, setting production goals, and dividing the farm's labor force to perform different tasks. Although Communist theory claimed that workers collectively owned the farms, workers only received wages, and profits went to the government.

Farmers whose families had owned land for generations were naturally opposed to having their property taken away. When independent farmers in Georgia (whom the Communists called kulaks, which means "tight-fisted" in Russian) refused to give up their land, Stalin dealt with them brutally. Soldiers evicted them from their homes, allowing them to leave with only the clothes they had on and no other personal possessions. Thousands of

"The Revolutionary Committee started a series of indiscriminate seizures and confiscations, without regard to class, and without taking into account the general economic and psychological state of [Armenians]."[11]

—Historian Bagrat Borian.

Workers harvest potatoes on a collective farm. People in the South Caucasus and elsewhere who had farmed the land for generations were forced to give up their farms to the government under Soviet collectivization.

farmers and their families were left broke and homeless, and thousands more were sent to places like Siberia to work in labor camps. Historians Carolyn McGiffert Ekedahl and Melvin A. Goodman write, "Stalin's war on the peasantry, the collectivization of Georgia's peasant farms [was] the most radical transformation of land tenure and village life in Georgia's history."[12]

In addition to the end of private ownership of farmland, the three South Caucasus nations experienced another radical change—a rapid, huge shift of their populations from rural to urban areas. This happened because the Soviets created industries in those countries to produce goods that other republics in the Soviet Union needed. Georgia, for example, became a center for manufacturing steel, chemicals, machine tools, and consumer products. Factories that produced those goods had to be located in cities, so the Soviets simply forced rural residents to move to urban areas to become industrial workers.

An example of this was Armenia. Once the most rural of the three South Caucasus countries, by the 1980s Soviet industrialization had shifted two-thirds of Armenia's population to urban areas. People involved often opposed such radical lifestyle changes. However, officials in Moscow made such economic decisions without regard to what individuals or the republics they lived in wanted or needed. Some republics benefited economically from Soviet rule, including Georgia, which was able to greatly expand its manganese mines in Chiatura with Soviet funds. However, Azerbaijan was robbed of the wealth its oil industry produced because profits were drained off by the Soviet government.

The Soviet Union's Communist economy was able to provide citizens with the basic necessities of life. This was mainly due to the intertwined economies of the Soviet republics. Some of the republics provided cheap natural resources to other republics so they could produce goods. For example, a republic that contributed cotton to make clothes would receive clothing in return. Thus, when the Soviet Union collapsed, the economies of all three South Caucasus nations fell apart because they had been dependent on each other for most of their economic transactions.

> "Stalin's war on the peasantry, the collectivization of Georgia's peasant farms [was] the most radical transformation of land tenure and village life in Georgia's history."[12]
>
> —Historians Carolyn McGiffert Ekedahl and Melvin A. Goodman.

A Tough Beginning

Armenia, Azerbaijan, and Georgia all had difficulties transitioning from Communist to capitalist, or free-market, economies. There were two reasons for this: South Caucasus countries had depended economically on other republics for decades, and knowledge of how to run private businesses had largely died with earlier generations.

Gross domestic product (GDP) is a term that calculates the size of a country's economy by totaling the value of all goods and services it produces in a single year. From 1990 until 1996 Armenia's GDP fell

annually. A worldwide recession after 2008 slowed growth, but the world's energy needs have kept Azerbaijan strong economically.

The huge amounts of money its energy sources have generated have created some problems for Azerbaijan as well as helping it financially. The biggest problem is that the wealth pouring into Azerbaijan is not shared by all. Corrupt government officials and executives in the energy business have grabbed most of the profits for themselves.

This corruption allegedly extends to the family of Ilham Aliyev, who succeeded his father as the country's president in 2003. News reports claim that Aliyev and his father before him used their power to enrich themselves in many of the nation's business deals. Aliyev's three daughters alone are said to own $75 million worth of real estate in Dubai, and other members of his family have been involved in deals that profited them greatly.

It is believed that corruption in Azerbaijan has limited the ability of many individuals and other segments of the economy to prosper. However, it is not the only South Caucasus nation to suffer from corruption.

> "The investments [from a 1994 oil deal with foreign countries] will open new possibilities for Azerbaijan and will ensure thousands of occupations for all people. It will be one of the greatest projects in the history of Azerbaijan."[14]
>
> —British Petroleum executive John Brown.

Georgia

Like other former Soviet republics, Georgia struggled economically after gaining its independence. Making matters worse was the political turmoil that forced the country's first two presidents—Zviad Gamsakhurdia and Eduard Shevardnadze—out of office. Georgia began rebounding economically after Mikheil Saakashvili became president in 2003 following the Rose Revolution that forced Shevardnadze to resign.

Saakashvili instituted economic reforms that simplified Georgia's tax system and lowered taxes for most average citizens, ended most gov-

Azerbaijan Oil

In July 2013 the State Oil Company of Azerbaijan Republic began drilling a new oil well 10,170 feet (3,100 m) deep into the Caspian Sea. The new well was expected to produce 100 tons (90.7 metric tons) of oil per day to add to the wealth Azerbaijan collects from the sale of its vast deposits of oil and natural gas. In a *New York Times Magazine* story just a few months earlier, reporter Peter Savodnik wrote that Azerbaijan has become one of the world's leading oil producers:

> In 2006, Azerbaijan started pumping crude from its oil field under the Caspian Sea through the new Baku-Tbilisi-Ceyhan pipeline. Now, with the help of [British Petroleum] and other foreign energy companies, one million barrels of oil course through the pipeline daily, ending at a Turkish port on the northeastern corner of the Mediterranean Sea. This makes Azerbaijan a legitimate energy power (the world's leading oil producer, Saudi Arabia, produces 11 million barrels every day) with a great deal of potential. If the proposed [new] pipeline, running from Turkey to Austria, is built, Azerbaijan would [also] become a conduit for gas reserves, linking Central Asia to Europe. This could strip Russia, which sells the European Union more than a third of the gas it consumes, of one of its most potent foreign-policy levers. It could also generate billions of dollars every year for Azerbaijan, which between 2006 and 2008 had the world's fastest-growing economy, at an average pace of 28 percent annually.

Peter Savodnik, "Azerbaijan Is Rich. Now It Wants to Be Famous," *New York Times Magazine*, February 8, 2013. www.nytimes.com.

ernment control of the economy, and made it easier for people to start businesses and engage in economic activities. Among Saakashvili's most important reforms were those that halted the corrupt practices that had been draining funds needed to strengthen the economy. The positive measures attracted needed foreign investment, which also spurred economic growth in Georgia. Today the country has a fast-growing economy based on Black Sea tourism, agriculture, wine making, and the manufacture of machine, chemical, and textile products.

But as in Azerbaijan, not all Georgians have shared equally in the nation's economic growth. Some of its citizens have benefited greatly with good jobs and high incomes, but unemployment—16.3 percent in 2010—and poverty—21 percent in 2009—have remained high. Poverty is even more widespread in rural Georgia, which suffers from a major economic gap compared with the country's urban areas.

Armenia

The South Caucasus nation that has had the slowest economic recovery since the breakup of the Soviet Union is Armenia. Ronald G. Suny, an expert on South Caucasus countries, says that Armenia struggled more economically than either Azerbaijan or Georgia. The problem was that

Irrigated fields in Armenia (pictured) produce large quantities of food. The country's agriculture industry now exports food such as grapes to other countries.

Armenia relied more heavily on the beneficial economic relationship that had existed among Soviet republics than did its South Caucasus neighbors. Armenia's products were exported almost exclusively to other Soviet republics, and 40 percent of its economy was based on military products those republics needed as part of the Soviet Union. That economic relationship ended with the demise of the Soviet Union.

Adding to Armenia's economic woes were two unrelated problems—a natural disaster and an ancient rivalry. Armenia was still recovering from a devastating 1988 earthquake that killed as many as forty-five thousand people and left half a million people homeless. And Armenia suffered from the ongoing financial burden of its territorial clash with Azerbaijan and the hostility the fighting created with Azerbaijan and Turkey. Its Islamic neighbors closed their borders to Armenia for purposes of trade, which hurt its economy by making it difficult to export or import products.

Armenia's eventual recovery was helped by the large number of Armenians living in other parts of the world. Expatriate Armenians provided investment funds that helped their homeland build a new economy. Also helping Armenia grow its economy was its tradition of quality education and a highly skilled workforce that under the Soviets had manufactured quality machine tools, textiles, and other products. Those positives enabled Armenia to begin rebuilding its economy, and since 1995 the country has shown solid economic growth.

Manufacturing remains the most important part of Armenia's economy; products include machine tools and instruments, electric motors, and trucks. However, it has also developed other economic sectors, including agriculture, mining (copper, zinc, gold, and lead), and tourism. Agriculture has grown since independence, mainly due to the nation's need to provide food for its own people after decades of receiving food from other republics in exchange for what it produced. In fact, Armenia now produces so much food that it exports food, such as grapes, to many countries. A negative for Armenia's economy is that it has to import most of its energy from Russia, including natural gas and nuclear fuel. Continuing corruption has also hurt its economy.

Despite some economic growth, Armenia is still the weakest South Caucasus nation financially. In 2010 nearly 36 percent of its people lived in poverty even though the government had increased pensions, which were low, and created new social welfare programs to help the poor. And jobs were so scarce in Armenia that thousands of workers, mostly men, were leaving the country each year to seek work. Many of those emigrating Armenians went to Russia, where wages were generally much higher, and they sent back so much money to their families that the funds have become an important part of Armenia's weak economy. In 2011 the money that flowed into Armenia from expatriate workers made up 12.1 percent of the nation's GDP.

South Caucasus Economies

Taken as a whole, the South Caucasus nations have recovered nicely from the economic devastation they experienced when the Soviet Union split apart. However, all three nations must still act to eliminate pockets of poverty that exist among their populations and do more to make sure everyone has a chance to benefit from their country's overall economic progress.

CHAPTER FOUR

South Caucasus Social Life

The various empires that controlled Armenia, Azerbaijan, and Georgia influenced their cultures and traditions. None of those empires had a greater impact than Russia, which ruled these countries for more than a century, first through the Russian Empire and then through the Soviet Union. The Russian Empire had practiced Russification, a policy of spreading the Russian language and culture to conquered countries. The Soviet Union treated its possessions similarly. Historian Theodore R. Weeks explains why Sovietization by the Communists was more successful in shaping the lives of people living in South Caucasus countries than the Russification efforts of the czars: "Sovietization aimed more ambitiously at a total transformation of human existence. [While] Sovietization never overtly advocated cultural assimilation, it did presume that Soviet citizens would use the Russian language as the primary language and expected Soviet citizens to adopt 'modern' lifestyles that often drew on Russian models."[15]

The Communists had a greater impact on those countries because their political system exerted more rigid control over the daily lives of its citizens and because its leaders were willing to use force to achieve their goals. Though the Soviets tried hard, they ultimately failed to change the cultural and social life of people in South Caucasus countries. This was especially true of the attempt to wipe out religious beliefs.

War on Religion

Religion—Christianity in Georgia and Armenia and Islam in Azerbaijan—had long played an important role in the cultural life of all three South

Caucasus countries. In Armenia, in particular, religion was a powerful source of national unity. Under Soviet rule religious teaching of any kind was prohibited, yet religion survived in all three countries.

The Soviets tried to stamp out religious beliefs because atheism was one of the tenets of Communist ideology. Communists believed religion blinded people to reality and weakened their faith in the state. Soviet authorities tried to make people abandon religion by making it difficult for people to worship. Communists sometimes punished both clerics and lay people by harassing or imprisoning them and making it more difficult for them to find work. They also tried to weaken religion by closing most churches and mosques; executing hundreds of Christian and Muslim clerics, who they feared would oppose communism; and persecuting people who remained active in religion. For example, Azerbaijan had about two thousand mosques when it became a Soviet republic. The Communists closed most of them during the 1930s, and by the 1980s only eighteen mosques were left in the entire country. The Communists did the same thing to churches in Georgia and Armenia. Government persecution forced people to worship privately, praying at home and secretly teaching religious lessons to their children to keep their faith alive.

"[While] Sovietization never overtly advocated cultural assimilation, it did presume that Soviet citizens would use the Russian language as the primary language and expected Soviet citizens to adopt 'modern' lifestyles that often drew on Russian models."[15]

—Historian Theodore R. Weeks.

In the 1970s, future Georgian president Zviad Gamsakhurdia was imprisoned for fighting for the freedom to worship in the Georgian Orthodox Church. Gamsakhurdia showed his deep religious beliefs again on April 9, 1991, the day Georgians voted to leave the Soviet Union. Attending church before he voted, Gamsakhurdia said, "Let everyone know that we were fighting for the restoration of the religious and national ideals of our ancestors. [Our] honest deed is protected by the Almighty, and therefore we will be victorious."[16] Since independence, hundreds of new churches have been built in Georgia and Armenia. Both countries included guarantees of religious freedom in their constitutions so people can once again openly practice religion.

In 2001 the Armenian Apostolic Church celebrated the seventeen hundredth anniversary of the nation's acceptance of Christianity. Garegin II, the church's leader, declared June 17, 2001, International Armenian Church Day to celebrate the church's survival. He was especially pleased by the effect the anniversary had on people who had not been to church in years. "The anniversary," said Garegin II, "has also brought unchurched people back to the church."[17] He said the church's new life could be seen by the gain of more than one thousand new teachers of Christianity, and a new cathedral dedicated to Saint Gregory the Illuminator being built in Yerevan would be the largest in Armenia.

Islam also survived in Azerbaijan during the Soviet era. However, seven decades of Communist oppression changed the way Azerbaijanis practiced their religion.

Women light candles during a prayer ceremony in Georgia. Soviet authorities prohibited religious teaching throughout the USSR, but religion survived in the South Caucasus and elsewhere.

Secular Islam

When Azerbaijan became an independent state in 1918, the Azerbaijan Democratic Republic was the first Muslim nation to have a democratic and secular, meaning nonreligious, form of government. Until then, religious leaders had wielded great power in governing Muslim nations. The republic allowed democratic elections of leaders and lawmakers and became the first Muslim nation to give women the right to vote, two years before US women won that right. Despite being able to vote, women were still considered inferior to men. They also had little personal freedom because of Islamic laws that allowed men to have multiple wives and marry young girls. It was also legal for husbands to kill their wives if they committed adultery under a practice known as blood vengeance. This practice is still permitted in some Islamic countries today.

During the Soviet era, the Communist war on religion focused on closing mosques and outlawing many ancient traditions associated with Islam. Some of those forced changes benefited women, including the end of polygamy and blood vengeance; a Soviet law in 1930 classified killing a woman as a counterrevolutionary act punishable by death. The attempt to eradicate Islamic traditions even changed the way people looked. Under the Soviets it became illegal for women to wear veils that Islamic law required, and men had to shave or trim long beards traditionally worn as a sign of religious fervor. The Soviets also closed civil courts run by Islamic clerics.

As in Christian Armenia and Georgia, Azerbaijan experienced a resurgence of religion when it regained its independence. But decades of religious intolerance under Soviet rule had changed the way people felt about Islam and the way they practiced it. Altay Goyuhsov, a professor of Islamic history at Baku State University, contends that Azerbaijan is the "most secular Muslim country in the world."[18] In Azerbaijan Islam does not play as important a role in the daily lives of people as it does for Muslims in other countries. Most Azerbaijanis never or only rarely attend services at a mosque and do not fast on holy days. Many Azerbaijanis also ignore Muslim prohibitions against drinking alcohol and eating pork.

The Soviet attempt to kill Islam weakened it, affected the way Azerbaijanis practice it, and downgraded its importance in people's daily lives.

How Religion Survived

One of the underlying philosophies of communism is that the state supersedes in importance all other institutions. Communists opposed Christianity, Judaism, and Islam because their followers believe God is more powerful and plays a more important role in their lives than the state. The attempts by Communists to crush religion forced Christians, Jews, and Muslims to practice their faiths in private because they feared being punished for their religious beliefs. Historian Tadeusz Swietochowski explains how Muslims in Azerbaijan did this:

> As a religion, Islam clearly suffered from the atmosphere of terror. With its rites no longer observed in public, Islam became privatized, confined to the family, the most conservative institution in Azerbaijan. Although women as a group had been the beneficiary of the Soviet secularization drive, having acquired an equality of rights, albeit more formal than real, they now unexpectedly assumed the role of guardians of native traditions, including above all the preservation of Islamic identity. At the same time, it was often deemed too risky to pass along the tenets of Islam to the young, who grew up unable even to say if their ancestry was Shia or Sunni. The prevailing adage became "keep religion in your heart," which was supplemented by another maxim, "say what is required from you and save your freedom of mind." This echoed an age-old response to religious and political oppression.

Tadeusz Swietochowski, "Azerbaijan: The Hidden Faces of Islam," *World Policy Journal*, Fall 2002, p. 69.

Islam did not disappear, however. "By every measure, Soviet rule proved the crucial test for Islam in Azerbaijan,"[19] says historian Tadeusz Swietochowski. Islam not only survived but is growing in strength again today. A 2012 survey of Azerbaijanis showed that the number of people who claimed religion was highly important in their lives had jumped from 28 percent in 2010 to 33 percent, and another 44 percent of respondents said it was an important part of their daily lives.

In addition to trying to stamp out religion, the Soviet Union tried with varying success to make Russian the key language in its republics. And Azerbaijan fared better in preserving its language than its religion.

War on Language

The Soviet Union required some republics to use Russian as their official government language but allowed most ethnic groups, including those in the South Caucasus nations, to continue using their native languages. However, most people in those countries wound up learning some Russian phrases and words to facilitate daily dealings with Russian party officials, government workers, and businesspeople. And South Caucasus citizens who wanted to take jobs in other parts of the Soviet Union had to learn to speak Russian because that was the common language workers in many professions used.

"By every measure, Soviet rule proved the crucial test for Islam in Azerbaijan."[19]

—Historian Tadeusz Swietochowski.

In 1978, when the Soviets tried to force Georgia to change its constitution to eliminate use of Georgian for government purposes, Georgians were so angry that they held a massive protest in the capital of Tbilisi on April 14. After thousands of angry citizens clashed with soldiers, Eduard Shevardnadze, the country's top Communist official, got the Soviets to allow Georgians to continue to use their native language. Ever since then, April 14 has been celebrated as the Day of Georgian Language.

However, there was nothing Georgia, Armenia, or Azerbaijan could do in 1978 when the Soviets ordered schools to teach Russian in kindergarten and nursery school. This offered the Soviets a way to get more people to learn and use Russian and reduce their reliance on native languages. The new law only partially succeeded. Even though more people learned Russian, they did not abandon their native languages. Historian

Svante E. Cornell explains what people did: "A type of double culture evolved, with the Azerbaijan Turkish language being confined to the home and social interactions, and Russian increasingly taking over the domains of officialdom, science, and technical language."[20] The same thing happened in Armenia and Georgia.

By continuing to speak traditional languages—including Azeri, the native Azerbaijan language—the South Caucasus nations saved them. During Soviet rule, however, Azerbaijan lost the traditional alphabet it had always used, which was based on Arabic script. In 1929 Soviet officials forced them to begin writing with the Latin alphabet used in most of the world, including the United States. A decade later, in 1939 Joseph Stalin forced Azerbaijan to switch to the Cyrillic script that Russia used; he did that partly to make it harder for Azerbaijan to have friendly relations with neighboring Muslim countries like Turkey. When Azerbaijan became independent, it switched back to a Latin alphabet to end decades of confusion over how to write Azeri, because it was a more common alphabet worldwide.

Industrialization Changed Lives

Soviet rule brought about changes to more than religion and language; it also changed the rural way of life that was common in South Caucasus nations before this period. In the first few decades of the twentieth century, countries around the world were undergoing a dramatic economic and social transformation known as industrialization. Advances in technology that allowed mass production of products from shoes to automobiles slowly shifted the world's economies from agriculture to manufacturing. The new jobs this created were located in large cities because companies needed large pools of workers and access to different types of transportation to receive raw materials and ship products.

When the Soviet Union was born in 1922, its republics, including those in the South Caucasus, had little industrial development; most people worked in agriculture and lived in rural areas. Stalin believed the USSR needed to create its own industries to manufacture its own products so that it would be self-sufficient and not have to buy them from other countries. To meet this goal, Stalin took steps to speed up industrialization in the Soviet Union.

The various republics experienced different types of industrialization. In Georgia the Soviets built many factories and hydroelectric power stations to power them. The Soviets also expanded mining operations in Georgia for coal and manganese, raw materials they could send to other republics. Similar industries were developed in other republics, and Azerbaijan's oil became more important than ever to power factories and the increased transportation that was needed. In order to achieve this industrialization, the Soviets forced millions of people to move from rural areas to cities where industries were concentrated. This massive population shift was most dramatic in Armenia, the most rural of the three republics. Between 1929 and 1939 the percentage of industrial workers grew from 13 percent to 31 percent of the workforce, and by 1935 industry supplied 62 percent of Armenian jobs.

A huge, Soviet-style apartment building is still in use in Yerevan, Armenia. The Soviet push for industrialization forced rural people to seek work in cities, and many lived in apartments like this one.

Soviet industrialization changed the way millions of people lived. Collectivization of agriculture forced millions of people to move to cities to work in factories and accept a lower standard of living. Self-sufficient farmers became workers dependent on employers for wages and who had to live in small, crowded apartments instead of their own homes. The emphasis on industry also led to widespread famine in the 1920s and 1930s due to decreased food production.

Accompanying the negative effects on the lives of many South Caucasus people were some positives. The Soviet system expanded and standardized education in countries that had once suffered from high rates of illiteracy. The Soviets also improved health care for people and provided a social welfare network that helped average people have better lives. These were the best and most positive effects people experienced under communism.

The negative and positive changes that came from Soviet rule drastically affected social life in the South Caucasus. Despite that, people in all three countries retained parts of the cultural identities they had forged over many centuries. However, those bits of cultural heritage now exist with and are sometimes mingled with cultural elements common to people around the world today.

> "A type of double culture evolved, with the Azerbaijan Turkish language being confined to the home and social interactions, and Russian increasingly taking over the domains of officialdom, science, and technical language."[20]
>
> —Historian Svante E. Cornell.

Old and New

Television, travel to other countries, and the Internet have brought elements of global culture, from entertainment to clothing, to people living in South Caucasus nations. That is especially true in big cities like Baku, Tbilisi, and Yerevan, where people have more opportunities to experience and learn about new things. For example, although traditional styles of folk music and singing are still performed in all three countries, they now have to compete with modern styles of music like jazz, rock and roll, and hip-hop.

People in Azerbaijan still enjoy mugam, a traditional music that combines poetry and complex instrumentals. However, Azerbaijanis also like modern music. Proof of their proficiency in today's popular music can be seen in their success in the Eurovision Song Contest, an annual televised competition in which selected entertainers from each country are allowed to perform one song. Azerbaijan won the 2011 contest when Ell and Nikki performed the pop song "Running Scared."

Traditional and modern forms of pop culture are sometimes blended to form an even newer style. An example is a hip-hop musical performed in Azerbaijan in 2011. *The Legend Returns* tells the classic love story of Leyli and Majnun that revered writer Nizami Ganjavi made famous in an epic poem nearly nine centuries ago. The musical, timed to celebrate the 870th anniversary of Ganjavi's birth, was set in today's world with hip-hop music and modern themes. Rapper Elshan Khose retained the context of the poem, and Irada Gozalova, who wrote the script, said, "We tried to convey this magnificent work to young people through the language of modern music."[21]

Food is another cultural area in which people combine the old and the new. Traditional Armenian food features lightly spiced meats, fresh salads, and *lavash*, a soft, thin flatbread that has become popular around the world. But in Armenia today people can also eat at fast-food franchises like McDonald's, Pizza Hut, and KFC. Nearly everyone in Georgia dines regularly on *khachapuri*, a cheese pie that is a traditional dish, but Georgians also go to Burger King for a hamburger and fries.

Despite their acceptance of many modern social habits, some of the oldest cultural traditions remain intact in the South Caucasus. One of Armenia's oldest customs is weaving rugs and carpets. In fact, carpet weaving is believed to have been born in Armenia nearly sixteen centuries ago. Both Herodotus, a fifth-century-BCE Greek historian, and Marco Polo, a twelfth-century traveler from Italy, mention the excellence of Armenian carpets in their writings. The carpets were so highly

Pop singers Ell and Nikki of Azerbaijan rehearse their song "Running Scared" at the 2011 Eurovision Song Contest in Germany. The couple won the competition.

prized that many of the empires that ruled Armenia demanded carpets as part of the taxes they assessed their Armenian subjects.

The artistic, highly decorative carpets made in Armenia are often hung on walls as artwork rather than used as floor coverings. Traditional Armenian rug designs still being used today feature a division of fields

Traditional Georgian Music

Even though many Georgians listen to modern popular music, traditional music is still well-loved there. Georgia has many types of folk music, much of it composed to accompany dances like the Kartuli, a graceful, romantic dance performed by just one couple that symbolizes love between a man and a woman. The most famous traditional singing is based on polyphony, which consists of multiple voices, usually three, singing or chanting lyrics in close harmony with each other. This type of music developed independently of European music. It is believed that Georgian polyphonic songs were sung as early as the fifth century. Polyphony and other traditional songs are often sung at public events, weddings, and other celebrations. They are sometimes called "table songs" because people sitting around tables often join in singing them. Travel writer Nancy McCaslin claims that as in other countries, traditional music has been an important way for Georgians to remember and honor their nation's past: "Georgian folk music shows diversity, warmth, strength, and passion. The songs, dances, and accompanying instruments have played an important role in keeping Georgian history and tradition alive through the centuries. They continue to be important today in helping the country's people better understand and honor their heritage."

Nancy McCaslin, "Music of Georgia," *Faces*, February 2007, p. 17.

that include medallions and artistic arrangements that employ geometric shapes. Many Armenian rugs contain cross shapes, human figures, and geometric bird and animal figures not usually found in rugs from other countries. The animal figures and crosses are believed to have originally had religious significance and are consistent with descriptions of rugs from Armenian manuscripts and visible in sculptures on Armenian churches and monasteries.

Cultures Survived

Communist rule in South Caucasus countries during the Soviet era influenced, changed, and sometimes eliminated centuries-old cultural traditions. But despite such heavy-handed and often brutal repression, some traditions remained intact. And since gaining independence, people in all three countries who are proud of their past and want to keep these traditions alive have returned to them and strengthened them so they will never be lost.

CHAPTER FIVE

The Future of the South Caucasus

In the two decades after Armenia, Azerbaijan, and Georgia regained their freedom from the Soviet Union, they succeeded in establishing themselves as independent nations with democratic systems of government. However, all three South Caucasus countries in 2013 were still dealing with a variety of difficult and potentially dangerous problems from the past that clouded their futures. Many of the area's problems today stem from religious, ethnic, and cultural divisions that have existed for centuries. Armenia and Azerbaijan remained at odds over the Nagorno-Karabakh region, which was once part of Azerbaijan but now claims its independence because its Christian Armenian majority does not want to be part of a Muslim nation. Armenia was also still dealing with a faltering economy. Georgia still had strained relations with Russia, which in 2008 briefly invaded it in defense of South Ossetia and Abkhazia, two regions that are seeking independence from Georgia.

The major issue facing oil-rich Azerbaijan was a facade of political stability after Ilham Aliyev was elected to his third straight five-year term as president on October 9, 2013. The problem with Aliyev's long tenure is that he and his family have become so powerful and wealthy that some people fear the Aliyevs might see themselves as a sort of royalty, destined to rule in perpetuity. The *Irish Times* and many other newspapers, for example, have used the word *dynasty* in headlines and stories about the fifty-one-year-old Aliyev's ever tightening grip on power.

Democracy or Dynasty?

Ilham and his father, Heydar, have held the office of president since June 1993. Heydar stepped down as president in early October 2003, and Ilham was elected to succeed him on October 15 with 76.84 percent of the vote. He was overwhelmingly reelected in 2008 with 87 percent of the vote and again in 2013 with nearly 85 percent of votes cast. Jamil Hasanli was one of several candidates who ran against Aliyev in 2013. Hasanli, who only got 5 percent of the vote, said he fears the Aliyev family will kill democracy in Azerbaijan: "I am running in this election with the paramount aim of ending twenty years of the Aliyev dynasty's misrule of my country, and restoring Azerbaijani democracy."[22]

Hasanli and many other people fear the Aliyev family has become too powerful. Aliyev's huge victory margins seem to indicate a stable democracy in which the vast majority of citizens voted for him. However, Azerbaijanis and international groups that monitor elections have claimed that his administration rigged the results in each of these elections.

In a story on the 2013 election, *Washington Post* reporter Max Fisher began by writing, "Azerbaijan's big presidential election [was] anticipated to be neither free nor fair."[23] His story included evidence the election had been fixed. Azerbaijan's election commission issued a report that Aliyev had won reelection with 72.76 percent of the vote. The problem with that, Fisher noted, was the commission released the total before voting began. When voting did end, officials declared Aliyev had won with 84.6 percent of the votes. However, the Organization for Security and Cooperation in Europe, an independent group that monitors elections for fairness, documented widespread voting irregularities and what appeared to be fraudulent vote counting. Marie Harf of the US State Department also claimed procedural irregularities tainted the election.

"I am running in this election with the paramount aim of ending twenty years of the Aliyev dynasty's misrule of my country, and restoring Azerbaijani democracy."[22]

—Azerbaijani presidential candidate Jamil Hasanli.

How Aliyev Rules

In addition to worries that Aliyev is manipulating the system to stay in power, Hasanli and others claim Aliyev is corrupt. That charge of corruption, which extends to his father, is believed to have made the Aliyev family fabulously wealthy. It is believed that both Heydar and Ilham Aliyev used their positions to enrich their family. It is hard to know how much money and property Aliyev has because ownership of his wealth is often hidden behind a series of secret corporations. However, news reports have connected his family to ownership or financial involvement in some of Azerbaijan's largest oil, construction, and communications companies. News stories have revealed that Ilham's teenage son owns nine mansions in Dubai worth $44 million. His two daughters also own $75 million worth of property in Dubai, which like Azerbaijan is an oil-producing nation in which royal families have become fabulously rich.

Domestic politics and war pose challenges for Azerbaijan. But the country's capital city Baku (pictured) seems well situated from its location on the Caspian Sea to move the country forward.

The massive wealth the Aliyev family has accumulated in a nation with an average yearly wage of just over $5,000 has made it extremely powerful. Aliyev has further strengthened his family's image and reputation by attaching the family name to many of the nation's most prestigious sites, including the Heydar Aliyev International Airport in Baku, Azerbaijan's capital. However, the main way Aliyev has managed to stay in power is by crushing any political opposition.

Human Rights Watch, an international group that investigates and supports human rights, claims Aliyev does whatever he wants to silence critics. During the 2013 campaign, Azerbaijan police and soldiers dispersed crowds taking part in protests against his policies. In April police in Baku arrested about 150 protesters for shouting that they wanted freedom and an end to Aliyev's rule. In July three youth activists were sentenced to fifteen days in jail for handing out stickers and leaflets in Baku calling for Aliyev's defeat. Such actions violate the right of free speech citizens in a democracy should have.

A 2011 US State Department report accused Aliyev of jailing political opponents and controlling the country's judicial system to punish them. He has limited freedom of the news media by harassing, jailing, and blackmailing reporters over negative stories about the government. He also controls the news by withholding funds from the State Support Fund for the Development of Mass Media to newspapers or television and radio stations that produce stories critical of government policies.

Threats to real democracy posed by Aliyev's wealth and power, however, are not the only problems Azerbaijan faces in the future. The country must also deal with high rates of poverty and unemployment in rural areas. And a problem from the past involving neighboring Armenia also remains unresolved—the status of Nagorno-Karabakh.

Azerbaijan's Other Worries

The Nagorno-Karabakh Republic is a disputed territory of 4,424 square miles (11,458 sq. km) that both Armenia and Azerbaijan have claimed since the end of World War I. During the Soviet era it was governed as a semiautonomous region within the Azerbaijan Soviet Socialist

Republic. On February 20, 1988, the parliament of Nagorno-Karabakh, located within the boundaries of southwestern Azerbaijan, voted to become part of Armenia. The attempt to withdraw from Azerbaijan ignited an undeclared war with Armenia in the mountainous region in question.

Sporadic fighting erupted into full-scale war in 1992. Armenians were victorious, and the war came to a halt on May 12, 1994, after the Russians got the two sides to agree to a cease-fire. Nagorno-Karabakh, which had declared its independence from Azerbaijan on September 2, 1991, functions today as an independent nation. However, Azerbaijan still claims the area, and there have been sporadic border clashes since then, including one in 2008 when sixteen soldiers died in a fight both sides claim the other started.

Cease-fire violations including incidents of snipers shooting at soldiers on the other side of the border have increased in recent years. Azerbaijan's increased military spending and statements by some officials that a military solution is necessary have renewed the threat of war. In 2013 Azerbaijan purchased $1 billion in weaponry from Russia, including tanks, artillery, and air-defense systems. And in June 2013 during an Army Day parade, Aliyev declared, "Strong Azerbaijan can afford to speak to feeble Armenia in any manner."[24]

Azerbaijan is better able to back up such warlike words than Armenia because it is much wealthier. And Armenia is confronted by other, more serious problems, including its faltering economy.

Armenia Struggles

Armenia fought Azerbaijan in 1988 and is willing to help the breakaway republic of Nagorno-Karabakh survive today because in its long history it has often had to battle Muslims for religious freedom. Armenian president Serzh Sargsyan, a native of Nagorno-Karabakh, argues that the Soviet Union's decision to make the area part of Azerbaijan defied tradition, and it should be independent today. In contrast to Azerbaijan's aggressive stance, Sargsyan is pursuing a peaceful settlement by asking other nations to help end the territorial dispute.

South Caucasus Pollution

Pollution is a legacy of Soviet dominance in all of the former republics. Authorities generally ignored damage that was being done to the environment; consequently, no attempts were made to stop it. Armenia, Azerbaijan, and Georgia have had mixed results in the last two decades in dealing with various environmental concerns. This has partly been because they have not had enough money to fix problems with air, water, and soil pollution.

Some of the worst South Caucasus pollution is in Azerbaijan and stems from oil production. Parts of Azerbaijan, including the Apsheron Peninsula near Baku and the Caspian Sea bordering it, are among the most ecologically damaged areas in the world. Due to oil spills from floating oil wells, the area suffers from severe soil and water pollution.

One of the biggest environmental concerns is clean water. The South Caucasus countries in 2009 joined together to plan how to clean up the Araks River, a tributary of the Kura River that flows from eastern Turkey into Azerbaijan. The Araks drains into a huge basin that provides water for people, agriculture, and industry in parts of Georgia, Armenia, and Azerbaijan. Chemical, industrial, biological, agricultural, and radioactive pollutants have heavily contaminated the river. Poor wastewater treatment plants have also polluted the water. The United States and European countries are helping the three nations clean up the river, but it will take decades to reverse the harm pollution has done to it.

Sargsyan was reelected to a second five-year term on February 18, 2013. Although his stance on Nagorno-Karabakh is popular, his victory with just 58.64 percent of the vote showed that many Armenians are unhappy with how he has governed. Charges of corruption have been leveled against Sargsyan's administration, along with claims of fraud regarding his reelection. There were mass protests in Yerevan, the capital of Armenia, and other cities over whether the election was fair, but they did nothing to stop Sargsyan from retaining his office.

A photographer captures a unique view of Armenia's capital city, Yerevan, at night. Unemployment remains a problem for Armenia, but Yerevan continues to expand its role as the country's administrative, cultural, and industrial center.

The biggest problem facing Armenia is its high unemployment rate—15.7 percent in 2012—due to a weak economy. A major factor inhibiting Armenia's economy is its poor relations with Muslim neighbors Azerbaijan and Turkey, which limits its ability to easily export and import goods. The economy is so weak that Armenia relies heavily on aid from the United States and loans from the World Bank and several other international financial institutions.

The lack of jobs has led tens of thousands of Armenian men to travel to foreign countries to find work to support their families. The money that workers send home totals nearly $2 billion a year, which is 20 percent of Armenia's domestic economy. Most workers go to Russia, where wages can be ten times higher than in Armenia. The lack of jobs is so dispiriting that in a 2013 survey, 40 percent of Armenians aged eighteen to thirty said they would like to leave the country in search of a better life elsewhere. And many people have already left Armenia.

Armenian Emigration

Historically, Armenians have always been willing to emigrate to escape problems ranging from Muslim discrimination to Soviet rule, which accounts for large Armenian populations in many European countries and the United States. A total of 49,600 Armenian citizens departed in 2012, and the continued emigration coupled with a low birth rate in Armenia has dropped its population from 3.5 million in 1991 to 3.1 million in 2013.

In addition to a decreasing population, the flow of men to other countries to find work is creating social problems. Ruben Yeganyan of the Caucasus Research Resource Center in Yerevan said absentee fathers are having a negative effect on families: "This is a social, demographic cost. Children don't live in normal families."[25] Making matters worse is that several thousand emigrant workers a year abandon their families after leaving Armenia.

In September 2013 the Armenian government took steps to improve the economy. Its 2014 budget increased pensions for retired workers by 15 percent and wages for government workers by 40 percent. Armenia has also been successful in getting aid from other countries, including the United States, which has given Armenia several billion dollars in aid since it became independent. At the same time Armenia has managed the difficult trick of remaining friendly with Russia, a political foe of the United States. Russia is not only its main energy supplier but also contributes aid to help the struggling nation.

Georgia has also received US help. However, its relations with Russia have been anything but cordial in recent years.

> "[Armenian fathers working abroad] is a social, demographic cost. Children don't live in normal families."[25]
>
> —Ruben Yeganyan of the Caucasus Research Resource Center in Yerevan.

War with Russia

Historian Ronald D. Asmus called the Russian-Georgian conflict the "little war that shook the world."[26] The war that lasted only five days began on August 7, 2008, when Georgia invaded South Ossetia to end

Georgia and Joseph Stalin

People in the Republic of Georgia are deeply divided on the subject of Joseph Stalin. The native Georgian once held immense power, but he was also responsible for the deaths of tens of millions of people. Although many Georgians hated Communist rule, some of them are proud that a fellow Georgian rose to such historic heights. A poll in 2013, the sixtieth anniversary of his death, showed that almost half of Georgians view him positively. His birthplace of Gori has a museum dedicated to Stalin that is a major tourist attraction. Olga Tochishvili has been a tour guide in Gori since Georgia was a Soviet republic. She claims that the feelings about Stalin differ depending on how old people are: "In Georgia, most of the old generation like Stalin. They think he was a great statesman, with his small mistakes. Young people don't like Stalin, of course. Our young people are not interested in history and they don't like Stalin." In 2013 Gori put back a huge statue of Stalin in front of his museum that had been taken down three years earlier.

Quoted in Bethany Bell, "Georgia Divided over Stalin 'Local Hero' Status in Gori," BBC News, March 4, 2013. www.bbc.co.uk.

a cease-fire that had begun in 1992. When the Soviet Union broke up in 1991, South Ossetia and Abkhazia tried to break away from Georgia and become independent nations. Russia in 1992 had brokered a cease-fire between Georgia and the two seceding regions, a move that left their status as independent nations in limbo with Georgia still claiming their territory as its own. Russia countered by sending troops into South Ossetia and launching air strikes against some military targets in Georgia.

The conflict ended with another cease-fire, reached with the help of US and European diplomats. The agreement ending the war did not decide the question of whether South Ossetia and Abkhazia should be independent, which is still undecided today. The brief war hurt Georgia economically by ruining relations with Russia, its biggest trading partner.

However, a change in government leadership in 2013 in Georgia is easing the tension between the two countries.

Mikheil Saakashvili, who spearheaded the Rose Revolution that improved conditions in Georgia, stepped down in October 2013 after a decade as president. That made Bidzina Ivanishvili, a billionaire businessman who became prime minister in October 25, 2012, the most influential political figure in Georgia. Ivanishvili heads a coalition called Georgian Dream that controls Georgia's parliament. The move to resume smoother economic and political relations with the dominant nation in the region is considered a positive for Georgia's future.

Ivanishvili's wealth—his net worth is estimated at $6.4 billion—helped finance the campaigns of candidates who made it possible for the Georgian Dream coalition to win control of Parliament. Their campaign centered on accusations that Saakashvili and his followers had brought back the economic corruption he had originally worked to end in Georgia politics. Ivanishvili also claimed that Saakashvili and his United National

A panoramic view of Tbilisi, Georgia's capital city, illustrates the mix of old and new that characterizes the South Caucasus countries. Ongoing tension with Russia and domestic politics pose challenges for Georgia.

Movement Party had weakened democracy by putting severe limits on freedom of the news media and using the judicial system and sometimes violence to punish political figures and groups opposed to their policies. Ivanishvili also drew popular support by promising to boost state investment in agriculture, lower income taxes for the poorest Georgians, and provide basic health insurance for everyone.

Georgia's economy has been boosted in recent years by tourism, which is one of the most rapidly growing parts of its economy. More than 3 million tourists visited the area in 2011, an increase of nearly 4 percent over the previous year. There are more than one hundred resorts in Georgia, including many on the eastern shore of the Black Sea, a popular vacation spot in that area of the world.

Georgia has also become an ally of the United States, something that was made easier by the fact that Mikheil Saakashvili was educated in the United States. Since 1992 the United States has given Georgia well over $3 billion in aid. It helped Georgia with $1 billion in humanitarian and recovery aid after its military brush with Russia in 2008.

> "The dramatic changes that have affected Azerbaijan [and other South Caucasus countries] society have brought with them completely new conditions of life for the younger generation of today as compared to previous ones."[27]
>
> —Author Svante E. Cornell.

South Caucasus Youth

The future holds many problems and opportunities for residents of the South Caucasus. No group is better able to solve or take advantage of them than young people born after the three countries became independent in 1991. Their lives have been very different from those of older people who grew up under Soviet rule. In a book about Azerbaijan, Svante E. Cornell writes, "The dramatic changes that have affected Azerbaijan society have brought with them completely new conditions of life for the younger generation of today as compared to previous ones."[27]

That statement also applies to Armenian and Georgian young people. In comparison with their parents and grandparents, who were raised in a closed Communist society, they have experienced more freedom in their daily lives and have been exposed to ideas and values from the rest of the world through mass media and the Internet. It is those young people, no longer shut off from life outside the South Caucasus, who will forge the future of Armenia, Azerbaijan, and Georgia.

SOURCE NOTES

Introduction: Gateway to Asia

1. Besik Urigashvili, "The Transcaucasus: Blood Ties," *Bulletin of the Atomic Scientists*, January/February 1994, p. 18.

Chapter One: Soviet Union Domination

2. A.O. Sarkissian, "Soviet Transcaucasia," *Foreign Affairs*, April 1936, p. 526.
3. Mike Wilson, "Armenia," *Faces*, September 1999, p. 8.
4. Ronald G. Suny, *The Making of the Georgian Nation*, 2nd ed. Bloomington: Indiana University Press, p. 207.
5. Aslan Amani, "Azerbaijani Democratic Republic, 1918–1920, the First Democracy in the Muslim World," Radio Oldar Urdu Azerbaijan, October 11, 2010. http://radioazerbaijan.ca.
6. Paul D. Steeves, ed., *The Modern Encyclopedia of Religions in Russia and the Soviet Union*, vol. 3. Gulf Breeze, FL: Academic International, 1991, p. 52.

Chapter Two: Political Life in the South Caucasus

7. Iurii Trifonov, "The Smashing of the Menshevik-Kulak Revolt in Georgia in 1924," *Russian Studies in History*, Fall 1977, p. 7.
8. Quoted in George Kennan, *Vagabond Life: The Caucasus Journals of George Kennan*. Seattle: University of Washington Press, 2003, p. 243.
9. Carolyn McGiffert Ekedahl and Melvin A. Goodman, *The Wars of Eduard Shevardnadze*. University Park: Pennsylvania State University Press, 1997, p. 10.
10. William E. Odom and Robert Dujarric, *Commonwealth or Empire? Russia, Central Asia, and the Transcaucus*. Indianapolis: Hudson Institute, 1995, p. 76.

Chapter Three: South Caucasus Economic Life

11. Quoted in Richard G. Hovannisian, ed., *The Armenian People from Ancient to Modern Times, vol. 2: Foreign Dominion to Statehood; The Fifteenth Century to the Twentieth Century.* New York: St. Martin's, 1997, p. 350.
12. Ekedahl and Goodman, *The Wars of Eduard Shevardnadze*, p. 10.
13. John Noble, Michael Kohn, and Danielle Systermans, *Georgia, Armenia & Azerbaijan.* Oakland, CA: Lonely Planet, 2008, p. 28.
14. Quoted in Nasser Sagheb and Masoud Javadi, "Azerbaijan's 'Contract of the Century' Finally Signed with Western Oil Consortium," *Azerbaijan International*, Winter 1994, p. 26.

Chapter Four: South Caucasus Social Life

15. Theodore R. Weeks, "Russification/Sovietization," European History Online, December 3, 2010. www.ieg-ego.eu.
16. Quoted in Elizabeth Shogren, "Nationalist Ideals Drive Georgian's Kremlin Battle: Zviad Gamsakhurdia, a Former Political Prisoner Who Is President of the Republic, Is Determined to Shake Free of Communism," *Los Angeles Times*, April 9, 1991. http://articles.latimes.com.
17. Quoted in Fred Strickert, "The Armenian Church Celebrates Its 1,700-Year Anniversary," *Washington Report on Middle East Affairs*, July 2001, p. 65.
18. Quoted in Shahla Sultanova, "Azerbaijan: Islam Comes with a Secular Face," EurAsiaNet, August 15, 2013. www.eurasianet.org.
19. Tadeusz Swietochowski, "Azerbaijan: The Hidden Faces of Islam," *World Policy Journal*, Fall 2002, p. 69.
20. Svante E. Cornell, *Azerbaijan Since Independence: Studies of Central Asia and the Caucasus.* Armonk, NY: Sharpe, 2010, p. 45.
21. Quoted in News.AZ, "Leyli and Majnun Hip-Hop Style," December 19, 2011. www.news.az.

Chapter Five: The Future of the South Caucasus

22. Jamil Hasanli, "Azerbaijan Must Use This Election to End the Aliyev Dynasty," *Guardian* (Manchester, UK), October 8, 2013. www.the guardian.com.

23. Max Fisher, "Oops: Azerbaijan Released Election Results Before Voting Had Even Started," *Washington Post*, October 9, 2013. www .washingtonpost.com.

24. Quoted in International Crisis Group, "Armenia and Azerbaijan: A Season of Risks," Brussels, Belgium, September 26, 2013. www.crisis group.org.

25. Quoted in Marcin Monko, "Pushed and Pulled Apart," *Transitions Online*, January 19, 2012. www.tol.org.

26. Ronald D. Asmus, *A Little War That Shook the World: Georgia, Russia, and the Future of the West*. New York: Palgrave Macmillan, 2010, p. 4.

27. Quoted in Cornell, *Azerbaijan Since Independence*, p. 46.

Geography

- Armenia is the smallest of the South Caucasus countries at 11,484 square miles (29,743 sq. km); Azerbaijan is the largest at 33,436 square miles (86,600 sq. km); and Georgia covers 26,911 square miles (69,700 sq. km).
- Azerbaijan borders the Caspian Sea; the Caucasus Mountains are to its north, and about half the country is covered by mountains.
- Georgia has many mountains; the Black Sea forms Georgia's eastern border, and Russia is its northern boundary.
- The Armenian plateau region is flat with many rivers and a few forests.

Population and Society

- Armenia has 2,974,184 people, of which 97.9 percent are ethnically Armenian.
- Azerbaijan has 9,590,159 people; 90.9 percent are Azeri, the ethnic designation for the country's original inhabitants, and 1.5 percent Armenian.
- Georgia has 4,555,911 people; 82.8 percent are Georgian, 6.5 percent Azeri, and 5.7 percent Armenian.
- Armenia and Georgia are Christian nations while Azerbaijan is Islamic.
- The official language of Azerbaijan is Azeri, of Georgia is Georgian, and of Armenia is Armenian.
- Mount Ararat is a national symbol of Armenia even though the mountain is in Turkey.

Government

- Armenia, Azerbaijan, and Georgia all have democratic forms of government.
- Ilham Aliyev has been Azerbaijan's president since 2003.

- The voting age in Armenia, Azerbaijan, and Georgia is eighteen.
- Georgia has nearly twenty political parties vying for control of legislative seats in its parliament.

Economy

- Azerbaijan has very low unemployment rates—only 1 percent in 2009.
- A major part of Armenia's economy is agriculture.
- Georgia's economy includes mining manganese, copper, and gold.
- Armenia has to import all its natural gas and oil.
- Azerbaijan produces nearly 1 million barrels of oil each day.
- Hydroelectric power provides most of Georgia's electricity; Georgia even exports electricity to other nations.

Communications

- Armenia has two public television networks and more than forty privately owned stations.
- Azerbaijan's telephone system is in need of modernization.
- Cellular telephone communication is more widespread in Georgia than fixed-line telephones.
- The Internet in Azerbaijan is largely unrestricted by the government.

Environment

- Azerbaijan's oil production in the Caspian Sea has created some of the worst air, water, and soil pollution in the world.
- Deforestation and military conflict with Azerbaijan has reduced Armenia's supply of wood to seriously low levels.
- Georgia suffers from air pollution in major cities, water pollution in rivers and the Black Sea, and inadequate supplies of safe drinking water.

Military

- Men and women can serve in Armenia's army and air force.

- Men in Azerbaijan aged eighteen to thirty-five are required to serve in the military, with terms of eighteen months for most but only twelve months for college graduates.
- Men and women in Georgia are eligible for compulsory or voluntary military service.
- Military spending by all three South Caucasus nations accounts for less than 3 percent of gross national products, with Georgia's the lowest at 1.9 percent.

Transportation

- The easiest way to travel to the South Caucasus countries is by airplane.
- People can travel within South Caucasus countries by trains, planes, automobiles, buses, and ferries.
- There are no border crossings between Armenia and Azerbaijan because of their hostile relationship to each other.
- Many villages in Georgia's mountain region are isolated during the winter because of a poorly developed transportation system.

FOR FURTHER RESEARCH

Books

Ronald D. Asmus, *A Little War That Shook the World: Georgia, Russia, and the Future of the West*. New York: Palgrave Macmillan, 2010.

Svante E. Cornell, *Azerbaijan Since Independence: Studies of Central Asia and the Caucasus*. Armonk, NY: Sharpe, 2010.

Nikki Kazimova, *Culture Smart: Azerbaijan*. London: Kuperard, 2011.

A.E. Redgate, *The Peoples of Europe: The Armenians*. Malden, MA: Blackwell, 2000.

Thomas de Waal, *Black Garden: Armenia and Azerbaijan Through Peace and War*. New York: New York University Press, 2003.

Websites

Azerbaijan International (www.azer.com). A website in English based in Los Angeles that bills itself as the world's largest about Azerbaijan.

BBC News Europe (www.bbc.co.uk/news/world/europe). This British Broadcasting Corporation site has information and stories on South Caucasus countries.

Countries Quest (www.countriesquest.com). Detailed information on every nation in the world, taken from Microsoft *Encarta*.

EurAsiaNet (www.eurasianet.org). The site has stories about political, economic, environmental, and social developments in the South Caucasus.

Library of Congress (http://lcweb2.loc.gov/frd/cs/getoc.html). This US government website has detailed information on Armenia, Azerbaijan, and Georgia as part of its studies of every country in the world.

New York Times (www.nytimes.com). The newspaper has articles and background information on countries from around the world.

World Factbook (www.cia.gov/library/publications/the-world-factbook). This Central Intelligence Agency site has detailed information about the history, people, government, economy, geography, communications, transportation, military, and other issues for 267 nations.